Mel Bay Presents

FORGET ME NOT

A Collection of 50 Memorable Traditional Irish Tunes

compiled, arranged and recorded in ornamented and unornamented versions

by Séamus Connolly and Laurel Martin

Pages 133, 134, and 135 have been intentionally left blank.

1 2 3 4 5 6 7 8 9 0

Visit us on the Web at www.melbay.com — E-mail us at email@melbay.com

We dedicate this book
to the memory of two dear friends:

Dr. Adele Dalsimer
1939 - 2000

co-founder of the Boston College Irish Studies Program,
who loved Irish culture
and always held the music in her heart

and

Tony Cuffe
1954 - 2001

fellow musician and teacher,
who encouraged us in the creation of this book
and whose love and courage inspired us all.

Contents

A Note From Kevin Burke

I first heard of Séamus Connolly when I was about ten years of age. I knew nothing about him except that everyone who heard him said he was a great fiddle player. A couple of years later I was fortunate enough to meet him. At first I was a little awestruck at being in the presence of such a wonderful musician but he quickly put me at ease and we played some music together. He was very kind and very complimentary about my playing, but, more importantly, he was very generous with his time and went to great lengths to explain things to me that he thought would help me become a better player. I was quite taken with the fact that he seemed so interested in taking the time to suggest ways of improving my music even though he hardly knew me.

I was very grateful for his advice and tried to incorporate it into my playing (but I must confess, Séamus, there was one piece of valuable information you gave me that I haven't got round to working on yet—any day now, I'll start on it. I promise!) Because of his generosity towards me when I was trying to learn more about traditional fiddle playing, and because of his enthusiasm for helping others learn, I was thrilled to hear that he and Laurel Martin were collaborating on compiling a music book. This book will be a great asset to anyone who has an interest in delving further into this kind of music, and I hope people will realize how much is owed to those who are willing to pass on to others their skill, knowledge and enthusiasm. This "passing on" is what Séamus and Laurel have done with this collection of music and I, on behalf of many others, would like to thank them for their generosity of spirit and for all the work they have done to compile this wonderful book.

Kevin Burke

Kevin Burke

Foreword

If your blood is stirred – if your spirit soars on the plaintive notes of Irish traditional music on the violin, pause here and reflect – because in this book and CDs you have a gift of unseen beauty.

It is a gift of music – and music from the heart too – brought to you by the virtuoso fiddle-master Séamus Connolly and his former pupil, Laurel Martin. Just as Séamus brought the old music of Ireland with him to the United States in 1972, so Laurel now passes it on to a younger generation in Boston.

Unbroken threads of tenderness...

Featured here, you will find wonderful tunes in the Irish tradition by distinguished living composers; you will hear echoes of the great music-makers of other days. And when their music comes to you, Laurel and Séamus will wish them to hover in spirit around your shoulders.

Life is such that it is only with the heart that we really 'see'; all you have to do here – open your heart to the 'call' in the music: listen, play or dance with it! Because it has, for generations, healed the pain of loss and dulled the drift of time, make your own of it now...

agus-

> *Gheobhair ceol na dtéad*
> *le luas na méar,*
> *Dod dhúisiú,*
> *is bhéarsaí grá...*

Tony MacMahon

Introduction

Several years have passed since we first considered the idea of compiling a collection of traditional Irish tunes to use in our teaching at Boston College. As our work on the book progressed, our vision of what it should become evolved beyond our original plan. We are pleased to present the resulting volume, *Forget Me Not: Fifty Memorable Traditional Irish Tunes*, and we hope that it will be useful not only to our Boston College fiddle students but to a wider audience of musicians as well.

As would be true for many traditional musicians, we commit the notes of our music to paper and ink with some degree of caution. The most captivating qualities of traditional Irish music may best be appreciated through listening. Notes on a page provide a mere promise of a tune; the expressive possibilities that come with phrasing, rhythmic emphasis, ornamentation and variation are difficult to capture in print. With these limitations in mind, we have tried to enhance the usefulness of this book by including two distinguishing features.

First of all, we have offered each tune in two versions. The first version is the most basic, and the second is printed with some ornaments and variations that are especially suited to the fiddle. The first version may be of particular interest to those who play instruments other than the fiddle, or to experienced musicians who prefer to learn the basic tune and then ornament it according to their own taste and style. It may also be helpful to less experienced musicians who are not yet ready to execute intricate ornaments. The second version is only a suggested arrangement; it is not meant to be definitive in any way. We encourage musicians using the book to look for the ways in which we move from the simple to the ornamented version and to use the same principles to create arrangements of their own.

Because we believe that listening is fundamental to the learning of Irish music, the second special feature we have included in this publication is a recording of each of the tunes in the book. Even those musicians who prefer to learn melodies from the written notes are urged to listen to the accompanying CDs, paying attention to subtleties of rhythm and phrasing that will not be found in the printed music.

With the help of many friends we have been fortunate to learn the sources and composers of some of the tunes we have included in this volume. We are grateful for the composers' generous permission to publish their music, and we acknowledge their authorship in the background notes that may be found in the final pages of the book. We would also like to express our gratitude to the many unknown and unnamed composers of tunes in this collection. The tune title "Forget Me Not," which we have chosen to use as the book's title, is a tribute to the contribution they have made. Although we may not know their names, the spirit of the old music they played and loved will not be forgotten.

We hope that you will enjoy learning and playing the tunes in this volume. Perhaps one day our paths will cross and we will have the pleasure of playing them with you.

Séamus Connolly and *Laurel Martin*

Acknowledgments

We would like to express our deep appreciation to the following people for their valuable support in the creation of this book.

For their generosity in allowing us to publish their compositions, we thank Joe Burke, Paddy Fahey, Brendan Mulhaire, Eddie Kelly, Micheál Ó hEidhin and Josephine Keegan. Special thanks to Neil Foley for permission to publish two compositions of his father, Con Foley ("Marian McCarthy" and "Planxty Penny").

For their assistance in locating sources, titles and composers of tunes, we are grateful to Anne Sheehy-McAuliffe, Nicky McAuliffe, Larry Gavin, Joe Burke, Jack Coen, Kevin Burke, Martin Connolly, Michael Connolly, Martin Mulhaire, Donncha Ó Múineacháin, Laurence Nugent, Randal Bays, Brian O'Kane, Paddy Cronin, Paddy O'Brien, Frank Harte, Paddy Reynolds, and Peadar O'Loughlin.

We are especially grateful to Elizabeth (Beth) Sweeney, Director of the Irish Music Center of the John J. Burns Library at Boston College, for her personal and professional support of this project. Our appreciation also goes to John Atteberry, Senior Reference Librarian and Bibliographer of the John J. Burns Library of Boston College, and to students Moira Walsh and Katie McCormick for their research assistance. For their interest in and support of this project we also thank Dr. Kevin O'Neill, Director of the Boston College Irish Studies Program, and Dr. Robert Savage, Assistant Director of the program. We also thank Dr. Philip O'Leary for his assistance with Irish spellings.

For their assistance in preparing the text, we thank Chrysandra Walter and David Martin. For proofreading of the text, our thanks go to Kathleen Guilday, Arwen Lietz and Elizabeth Sweeney.

We are grateful to David Lang for the front cover artwork, and to Jimmy Hogan, Betsy Sullivan and Nathaniel Martin, whose images appear on the cover. We also extend our thanks to Jim Higgins and Joan Ross for the photos.

We offer our special thanks to accordionist Joe Derrane for his expertise and help with proofreading the musical text.

For his gracious words and thoughts in the foreword of the book, we are deeply grateful to Anthony (Tony) MacMahon. We also offer our special thanks to Kevin Burke for the note that appears in the early pages of the book. Our thanks also go to Joe Wilson of the National Council for the Traditional Arts, and to Earle Hitchner, music writer for the *Irish Echo, Irish Music, The Wall Street Journal,* and *SonicNet,* for their kind support.

For his patience and professionalism in his work on the musical transcriptions, and for his support and advice, we thank John McGann.

To the many friends who have encouraged us along the way, your caring and interest have been greatly appreciated. We would especially like to express our warm gratitude to the following friends and musicians who offered guidance and suggestions as our work on the book unfolded: Tony Cuffe, Kathleen Guilday, Jimmy Noonan, Larry Reynolds, and Alice Josephs. We also thank the many fiddle students we have taught through the years. Their dedication and enthusiasm for the music are an endless source of inspiration to us.

Above all, we offer our loving gratitude to members of our families — Chrysandra Walter, David, Sarah and Nathaniel Martin, and Doris and Albert Koch. Their constant moral support, hard work and patience made all the difference in the world to us. ***Thank you!***

About the Recording

We would like to thank the following people for assisting us in the production of the *Forget Me Not* recording: Bob Lawson and sound engineers Mark Wessel and Will Sandalls of Blue Jay Recording Studio, Toby Mountain of Northeastern Digital Recording, Inc., Lydia Shaw and Ann Sullivan for their studio assistance, and Bob Childs.

We are grateful and honored to be joined on the final tracks of CD #2 by our friends Joe Derrane, John McGann, Jimmy Noonan, and Beth Sweeney. We are also proud to introduce the following young musicians and students (ages 9-18) who join us on the tracks listed below: Nathaniel Martin, Lydia Shaw, Betsy Sullivan, Sarah Thomae, and Jessye Weinstein.

CD #2, track 45 — hornpipe / jig: *Astley's / Eddie Moloney's Jig*
Accordion: Joe Derrane
Fiddles: Séamus Connolly, Laurel Martin, Lydia Shaw, and Sarah Thomae
Flute: Jimmy Noonan
Keyboard: Beth Sweeney
Mandolin: John McGann

CD #2, track 46 — reels: *Hickey's / Mick Collins' / Lad O'Beirne's*
Fiddles: Séamus Connolly, Laurel Martin, Lydia Shaw, and Sarah Thomae

CD #2, track 47 — reels: *John Kelly's Concertina Reel / Kiss the Bride / Martin Ansboro's*
Accordion: Joe Derrane
Flute: Jimmy Noonan
Fiddles: Séamus Connolly, Laurel Martin, Lydia Shaw, Beth Sweeney, and Sarah Thomae
Guitar: John McGann

CD #2, track 48 — jigs: *The Hare in the Corn / Kiss Me Sweetheart*
Fiddles: Séamus Connolly, Laurel Martin, Lydia Shaw, Betsy Sullivan, Sarah Thomae, and Jessye Weinstein
Flute: Jimmy Noonan
Keyboard: Beth Sweeney
Uilleann Pipes: Nathaniel Martin

The enclosed two CD recordings were arranged, recorded and produced by Séamus Connolly and Laurel Martin at Blue Jay Recording Studio, Carlisle, Massachusetts. Digital editing and mastering at Northeastern Digital Recording, Southborough, Massachusetts.

On all duet tracks Séamus and Laurel play violins made by Robert M. Childs of Cambridge, Massachusetts (http://www.maestronet.com/robertmchilds).

Index of Tunes

Astley's

Hornpipe

Astley's

Hornpipe

Brendan Mulhaire's

Reel

Composed by Brendan Mulhaire

Brendan Mulhaire's

Reel

Composed by Brendan Mulhaire

15

Bridge of Athlone

Hornpipe

CD #1, Track #5

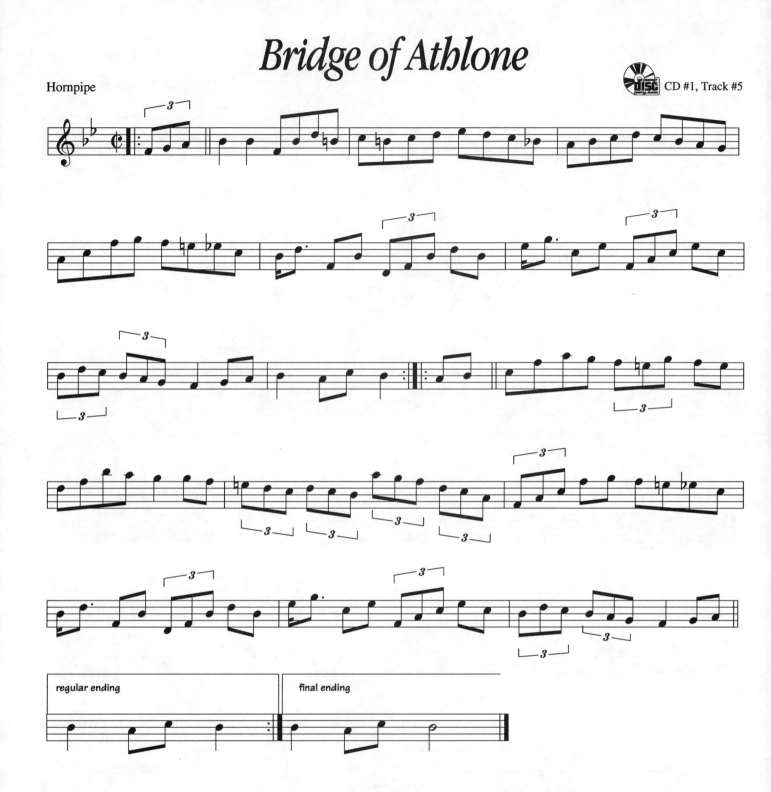

16

Bridge of Athlone

Hornpipe

CD #1, Track #6

The Collier's

Reel

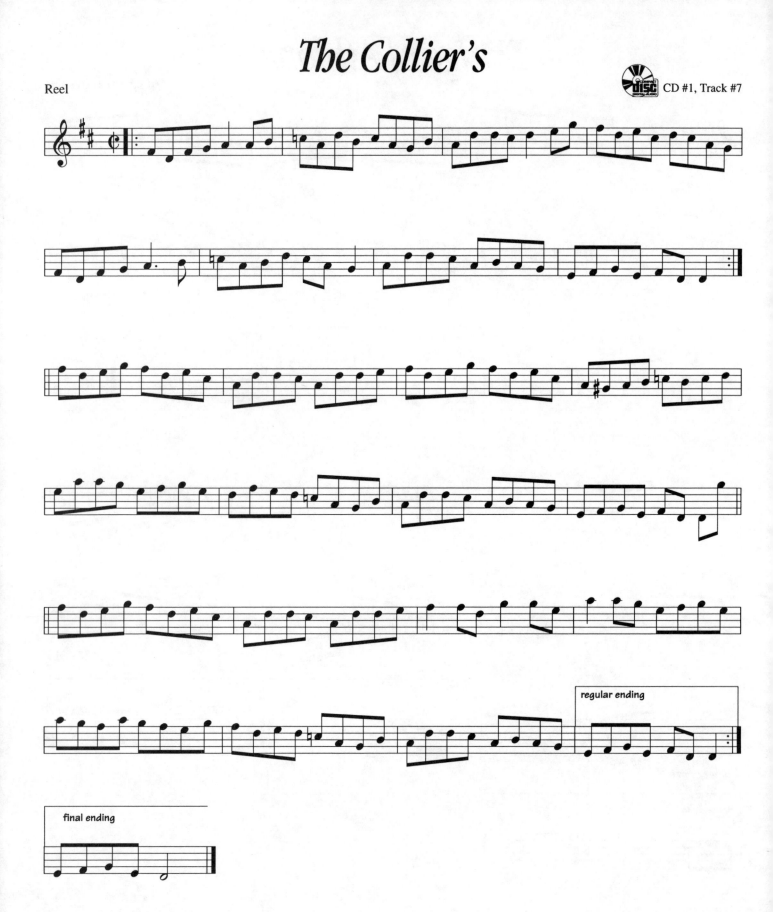

regular ending

final ending

The Collier's

Reel

Connolly's

Jig

regular ending

final ending

Connolly's

CD #1, Track #10

regular ending

final ending

The Doon

Reel

The Doon

Reel

final ending

Eddie Moloney's

Jig

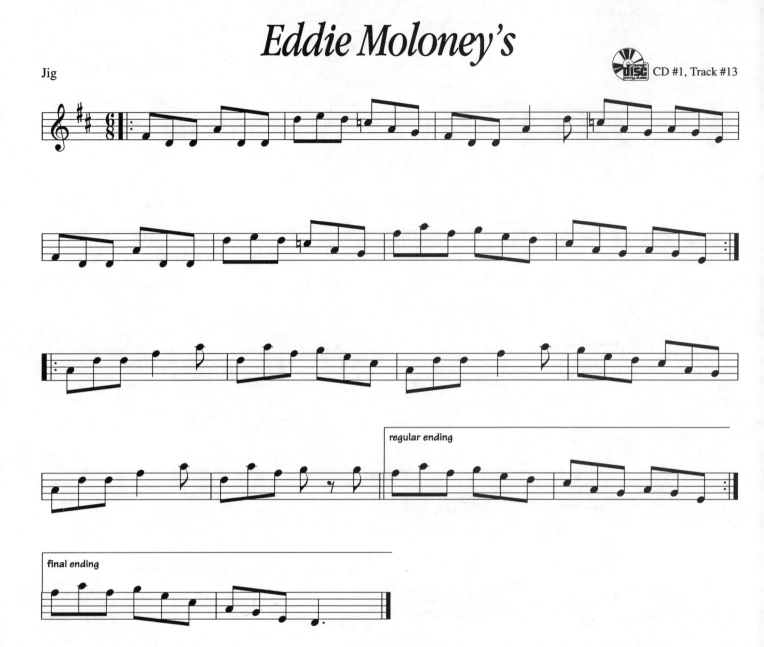

regular ending

final ending

Eddie Moloney's

CD #1, Track #14
CD #2, Track #45

Jig

regular ending

final ending

Eddie Moloney's Favourite

Jig

Eddie Moloney's Favourite

Jig

regular ending   final ending

The Fairhaired Boy

Jig

The Fairhaired Boy

Jig

Fare Thee Well Sweet Killaloe

March

regular ending

final ending

Fare Thee Well Sweet Killaloe

March

CD #1, Track #20

regular ending

final ending

Father Fielding's Favourite

Jig

regular ending

final ending

Father Fielding's Favourite

Jig

Forget Me Not

Reel

Composed by Larry Redican

Forget Me Not

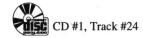
Reel

Composed by Larry Redican

The Good Woman's Lament for O'Connell

Air

CD #1, Track #25

regular ending

final ending

The Good Woman's Lament for O'Connell

Air

regular ending

final ending

The Great Northern Bands

March

regular ending   final ending

The Great Northern Bands

March

regular ending

final ending

The Hare in the Corn

Jig

CD #1, Track #29

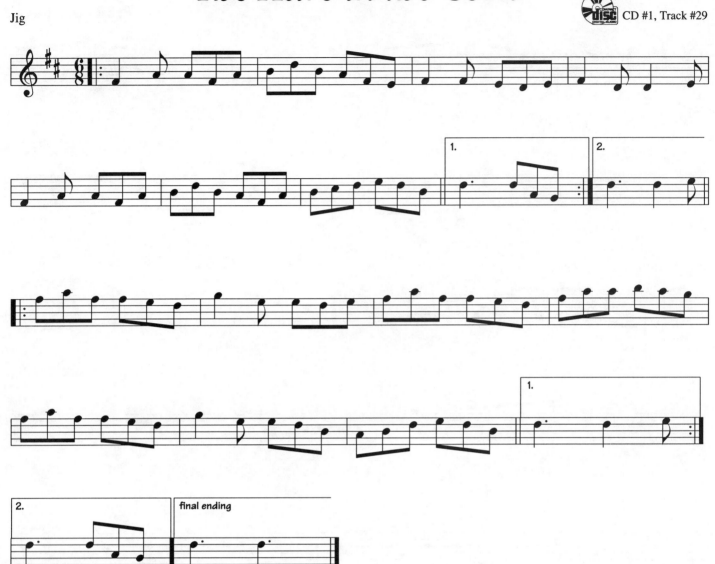

40

The Hare in the Corn

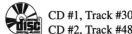

Jig

Hickey's

Reel

Hickey's

Reel

Humours of Castle Bernard

Hornpipe

CD #1, Track #33

regular ending

final ending

Humours of Castle Bernard

Hornpipe

Jimmy O'Brien's

Jig

Jimmy O'Brien's

CD #1, Track #36

regular ending

final ending

John Kelly's Concertina Reel

regular ending

final ending

John Kelly's Concertina Reel

Reel

regular ending

final ending

Kathleen Lawrie's Wedding

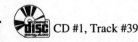

Reel

Composed by Josie McDermott

regular ending

final ending

Kathleen Lawrie's Wedding

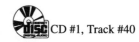

CD #1, Track #40

Reel

Composed by Josie McDermott

Kathleen O'Shea's or Ben Hill

Hornpipe

CD #1, Track #41

Kathleen O'Shea's or Ben Hill

Hornpipe

Kiss Me Sweetheart

Single Jig

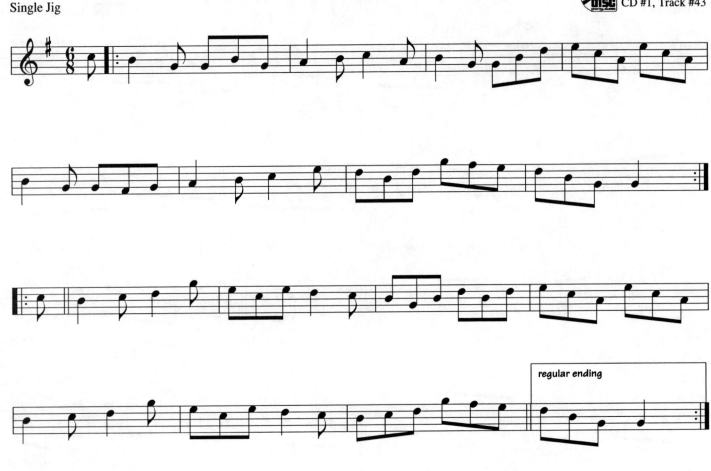

regular ending

final ending

Kiss Me Sweetheart

Single Jig

regular ending

final ending

Kiss the Bride

Reel

Kiss the Bride

Reel

regular ending

final ending

The Knockawhinna

CD #1, Track #47

Jig

Composed by Mícheál ÓhEidhin

The Knockawhinna

Jig

Composed by Mícheál ÓhEidhin

Lad O'Beirne's

CD #1, Track #49

Reel

Lad O'Beirne's

Reel

61

Marian McCarthy

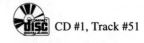

Set Dance

Composed by Con Foley

Marian McCarthy

 CD #1, Track #52

Set Dance

Composed by Con Foley

Martin Ansboro's

Reel

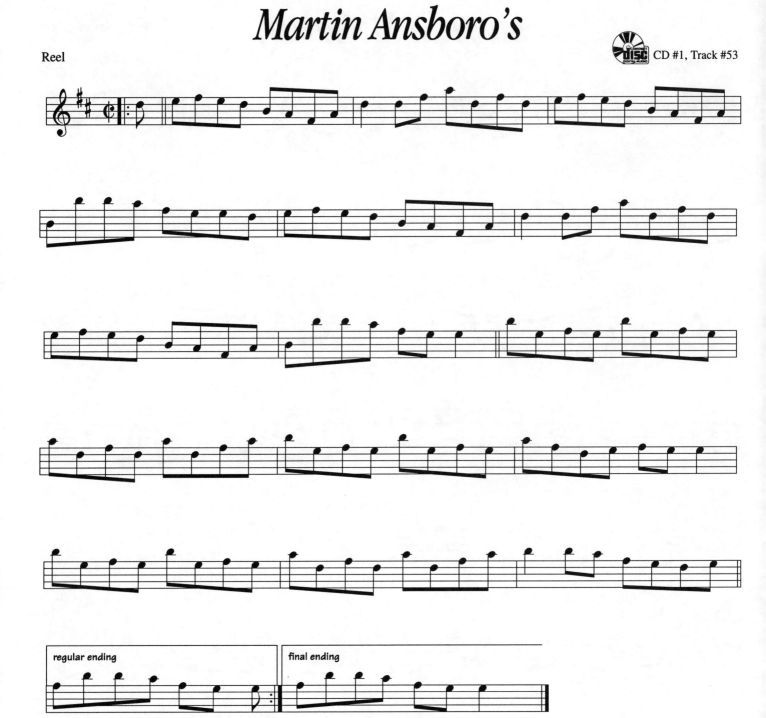

Martin Ansboro's

Reel

regular ending

final ending

The Meelick Team (D minor)

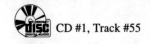
CD #1, Track #55

Jig

Composed by Eddie Kelly

regular ending

final ending

The Meelick Team (D minor)

CD #1, Track #56

Jig

Composed by Eddie Kelly

regular ending

final ending

The Meelick Team (E minor)

 CD #1, Track #57

Jig

Composed by Eddie Kelly

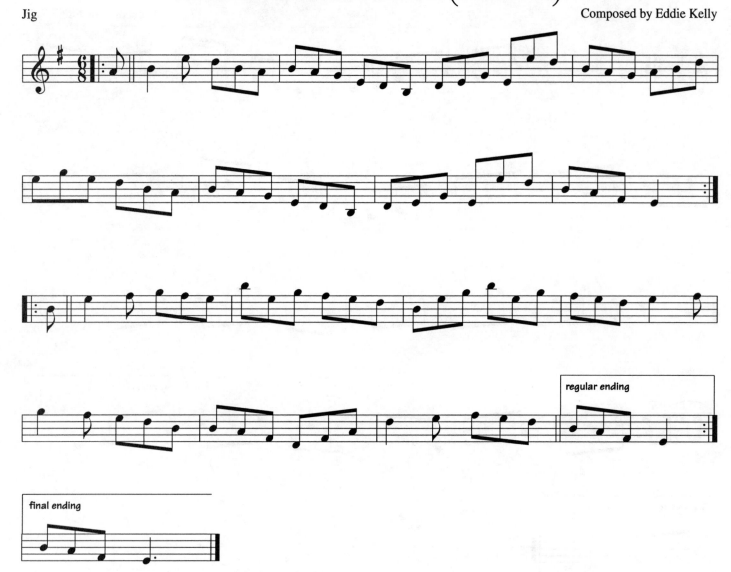

The Meelick Team (E minor)

CD #1, Track #58

Jig

Composed by Eddie Kelly

regular ending

final ending

Mick Collins'

Reel

regular ending

final ending

Mick Collins'

Reel

regular ending

final ending

Minnie Foster's

CD #2, Track #3

Hornpipe

Minnie Foster's

CD #2, Track #4

Hornpipe

regular ending

final ending

Molly on the Shore

Molly on the Shore

Reel

Alternative 3rd part

regular ending

final ending

The Morning Mist

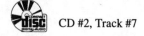

Reel

Composed by Joe Burke

The Morning Mist

Reel

Composed by Joe Burke

regular ending

final ending

The Mountain Top

Reel

The Mountain Top

Reel

Murphy's

Reel

Murphy's

CD #2, Track #12

Reel

No Surrender

Jig March

regular ending

final ending

No Surrender

Jig March

CD #2, Track #14

The Old Blackbird

Hornpipe

The Old Blackbird

Hornpipe

CD #2, Track #16

The Old Cross

March

The Old Cross

March

The Old Dudeen

Reel

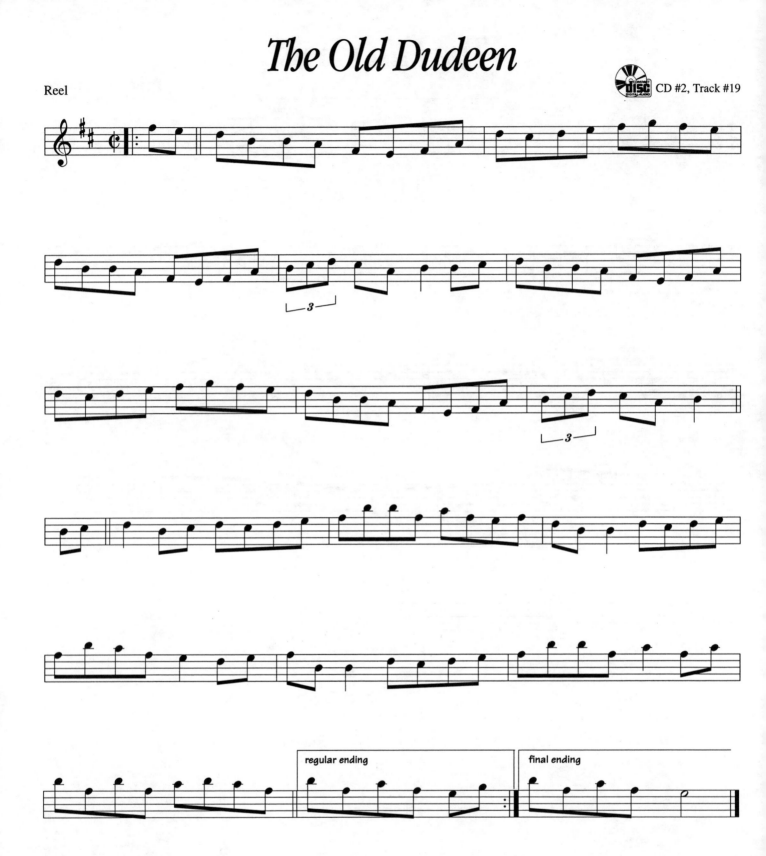

The Old Dudeen

CD #2, Track #20

Reel

Old Ireland a Long Farewell

Air

regular ending

final ending

Old Ireland a Long Farewell

Air

CD #2, Track #22

regular ending

final ending

O'Reilly's Greyhound

Reel

O'Reilly's Greyhound

Reel

Paddy Fahey's

CD #2, Track #25

Reel

Composed by Paddy Fahey

Paddy Fahey's

 CD #2, Track #26

Composed by Paddy Fahey

Reel

Paddy Kelly's

Reel

Composed by Paddy Kelly

Paddy Kelly's

CD #2, Track #28

Reel

Composed by Paddy Kelly

regular ending

final ending

Pigeon on the Gate

Single Jig

CD #2, Track #29

Pigeon on the Gate

Single Jig

CD #2, Track #30

Planxty Penny

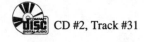 CD #2, Track #31

Set Dance

Composed by Con Foley

Planxty Penny

Set Dance

Composed by Con Foley

The Second Wedding

Reel

regular ending

final ending

The Second Wedding

CD #2, Track #34

Reel

Sixmilebridge

CD #2, Track #35

Reel

final ending

Sixmilebridge

Reel

CD #2, Track #36

final ending

The Spindle Shanks

Reel

regular ending

final ending

The Spindle Shanks

Reel

CD #2, Track #38

107

The Tempest

Reel

CD #2, Track #39

The Tempest

The Thrush in the Bush

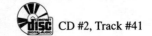 CD #2, Track #41

Jig

Composed by Josephine Keegan

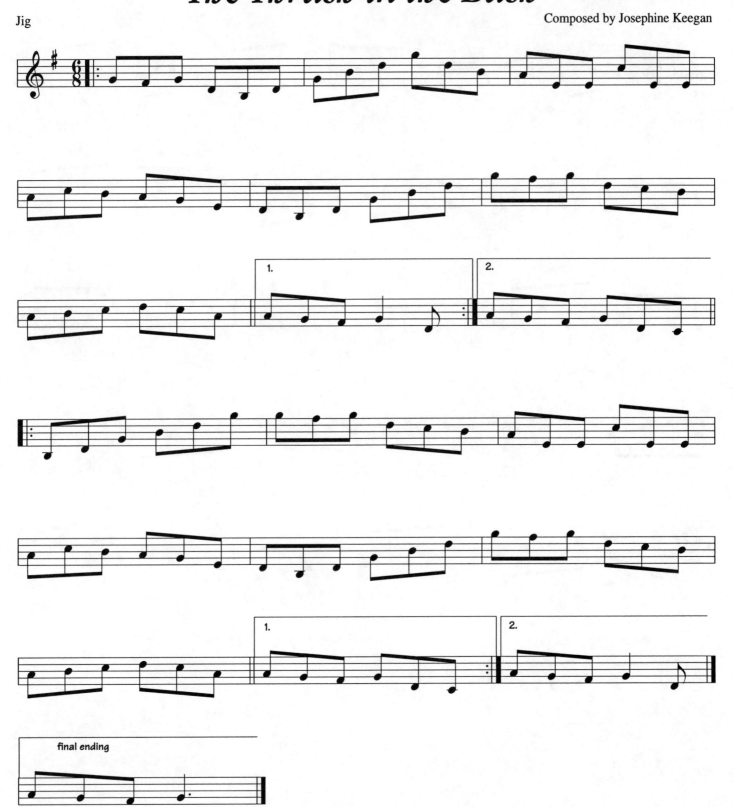

The Thrush in the Bush

Jig

Composed by Josephine Keegan

Tommy Mulhaire's

Jig

Composed by Tommy Mulhaire

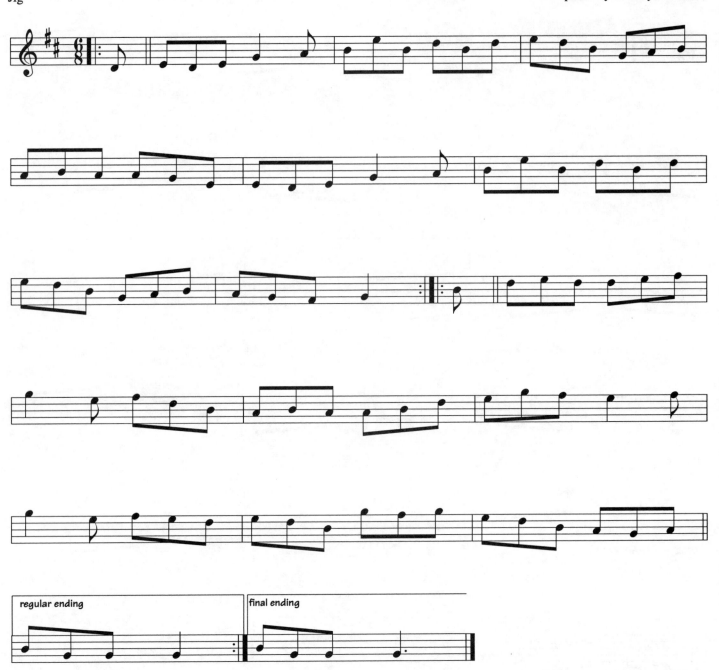

Tommy Mulhaire's

CD #2, Track #44

Jig

Composed by Tommy Mulhaire

Background Information

And personal reminiscences of the tunes as told by Séamus Connolly

Astley's (Hornpipe)

For as long as I can remember, Raidió Éireann has been broadcasting *Céilí House*, a Saturday night programme of Irish music and song. For many years the late and inimitable Seán Ó Murchú was the programme's compere as it was transmitted live from the Dublin Studios. Mr. Ó Murchú presented a different céilí band each week, along with visiting guest musicians and singers from around Ireland and England. It was on *Céilí House* that I first heard "Astley's Hornpipe" played by the Eamonn Ceannt Céilí Band from Dublin. The band was regularly featured on Mr. Ó Murchú's programme and they always had a "knack" of coming up with tunes that were seldom heard.

The leader of the Eamonn Ceannt Céilí Band was Viola Preston, a piano accordion player from Co. Sligo. Viola was a sister of Boston flute player Eugene (Gene) Preston, affectionately known as "the Boss" by Irish musicians in the Boston area. Viola and Gene were aunt and uncle to flute player Michael Preston (former member of the Tulla Céilí Band), who now lives in New York.

The ever-popular *Céilí House* is still being broadcast today, and Radio Telefís Éireann's web site (http://www.rte.ie/) transmits *Céilí House* around the world. The programme, now hosted by banjo player Kieran Hanrahan, has a new format, and is produced and pre-recorded at different locations throughout Ireland for later transmission. While in Boston as a visiting professor at the 1999 Boston College Gaelic Roots Summer School, Kieran recorded a *Céilí House* programme featuring many of the visiting faculty who were teaching during that week in June.

Brendan Mulhaire's (Reel)

I learned this tune from my good friend, accordion master Joe Burke of Loughrea, Co. Galway, almost 40 years ago. Joe didn't have a name for it but thought it might be a composition of Martin Mulhaire's. During a conversation with another friend and Irish music authority, Paddy O'Brien of Co. Offaly (currently of Minneapolis), I learned that Paddy, too, believed it to be a Martin Mulhaire tune. When I contacted Martin, he informed me that it was his brother Brendan's composition. We are grateful to Brendan Mulhaire for allowing us to publish this lovely tune. He never did name it, hence its title!

Bridge of Athlone (Hornpipe)

The Bridge of Athlone crosses the lordly River Shannon and connects the province of Connaught to the province of Leinster. History tells us that during the Williamite Army's

114

march through Ireland in 1691, General Ginkell, who commanded the English army, made numerous attempts in June of that year to cross over the bridge into Connaught in an effort to reach the Irish town side of Athlone.

Lieutenant General St. Ruth had arrived at the Shannon River six weeks earlier with a French fleet carrying provisions, arms and ammunition for a now divided Irish army. St. Ruth had by this time taken command of the Irish troops, and gave orders to burn the bridge, but Ginkell and his men outnumbered St. Ruth's army. After serious Irish casualties, the Williamite Army crossed the majestic Shannon into Connaught.

My memories of the Bridge of Athlone are musical and happier. During summer holidays from school I would travel the River Shannon with my father, who was skipper of a tugboat that sailed between Limerick and Athlone. I looked forward to these trips on the river because they gave me an opportunity to meet other musicians when, at night, we would dock at various ports-of-call. My favourite port was Athlone because I knew that when we got there I would have an opportunity to meet and play with some of the local musicians, including Paul Brock, who, at age 14, was known as a "boy wonder."

Many years have passed since the Siege of Athlone. The water continues to run deep under the bridge and the music continues to be played. Paul is still making a name for himself through performances and recordings. He and I never did have an opportunity to play this great tune together. We first heard it played on a 78-rpm recording by the legendary maestro fiddler, Michael Coleman. Today I enjoy listening to a digital performance of the hornpipe played by another maestro and legend, Joe Derrane from Boston. Joe's recording, *Return to Inis Mor*, with Carl Hession on piano, was released on the Green Linnet label in 1996.

The Collier's (Reel)

I first heard this reel played by the great uilleann piper, pipe maker, and teacher, Leo Rowsome from Dublin. I'm not sure where the tune originated but it may have come from the coal mining and musical area of Arigna in Co. Leitrim. "The Collier's" may also have its origins in England's Tyneside industrial music and song traditions.

Music and song have long been an important part of life in the coal mining community of Tyneside. After Ireland's great hunger of 1845, the Irish people who immigrated to England and made their homes along the River Tyne brought the music and songs of Ireland with them. Tyneside's thriving musical culture and traditions were undoubtedly enhanced by these immigrant Irish workers, who themselves learned many fine tunes, songs, and Northumbrian traditions from the local culture along the River Tyne.

"The Collier's" has become a standard at music sessions everywhere. Laurel and I have included a variation (sometimes forgotten) at the end of the second B part.

Connolly's (Jig)

While doing research in the library at Trinity College Dublin in 1981, I came across this jig in a collection of Irish dance tunes. I was delighted when the librarian gave me a copy of the tune. Looking at it later, I discovered that the second part of the jig was missing the last two measures, and I could not recall from which book the tune was copied. In order to make it complete, I made up two measures and added them at the end of my copy. I then had for myself what I thought to be a lovely two-part jig.

I had concerns about including the tune in this collection because of the missing measures. I mentioned this to my colleague and friend Beth Sweeney, director of the Irish Music Archives at Boston College. Beth located the tune in P.W. Joyce's 1909 collection, *Old Irish Folk Music and Songs*, and found a lovely third part to the jig printed on the opposite page. Laurel and I are delighted to know that "Connolly's" has always been a great three-part jig. (We wish we knew who Connolly was!!)

The Doon (Reel)

We learned this reel from a 78-rpm Copley recording of master fiddler Paddy Cronin. He played this tune with another reel, which he called "Quinn's," sometimes known as "The Mountain Top." We have also included "The Mountain Top" in this collection. Paddy came to America in 1949 and lived in the Boston area for more than forty years. He made a number of recordings for Copley Records, some of which may be found at the Boston College Irish Music Archives. Paddy returned to his native Co. Kerry in the early 1990s.

Eddie Moloney's (Jig)

The late Eddie Moloney has always been one of my favourite flute players. Eddie lived in Galway City, but originally came from the area around Ballinakill, Co. Galway, a place famous for its flute and fiddle players. Eddie had an amazing repertoire of tunes peculiar to his part of the country, including this jig and "Eddie Moloney's Favourite," which is also printed in this collection. Eddie's flute playing can be heard on a number of long-playing records recorded by Mulhaire's Céilí Band and the Shaskeen Céilí Band.

Eddie Moloney's Favourite (Jig)

I first heard this jig played by Mulhaire's Céilí Band in the early 1960s in Lixnaw, Co. Kerry at one of the late Diarmuid Ó Catháin's (better known to his friends as Jerry Keane) famous all-star concerts. Jerry was an authority on Irish music and an All-Ireland melodeon champion. He served for three years as national president of Comhaltas Ceoltóirí Éireann, formed in 1951 for the preservation and enhancement of traditional Irish music. Diarmuid was the first person in Co. Kerry to bring such outstanding musicians as Eddie Moloney, Tommy and Brendan Mulhaire, Willie Clancy, Joe Burke, Paddy Carty, Paddy Canny, Peadar O'Loughlin, Paddy O'Brien (Tipperary) and others to perform for the people of his native village of Lixnaw and for a wider Munster audience. Diarmuid (Jer) will be remembered for his enormous contribution to the culture of Ireland.

The Fairhaired Boy (Jig)

My good friend and master accordionist Anthony (Tony) MacMahon, from my native Co. Clare, brought this tune to my attention in the early 1960s. As guest musician on Raidió Éireann's *Céilí House,* he played this jig along with a well-known tune called "Father O'Flynn." A version of "The Fairhaired Boy" can be found in Captain Francis O'Neill's collection, *The Dance Music of Ireland: 1001 Gems*, published in Chicago in 1907.

Tony has numerous recordings to his credit, and Laurel and I are delighted that he has recently released a new CD recording titled *MacMahon from Clare.*

Fare Thee Well Sweet Killaloe (March)

A version of this tune appears in P.W. Joyce's *Old Irish Folk Music and Songs* (1909). The tune can also be found in Francis O'Neill's *Music of Ireland: Eighteen Hundred and Fifty Melodies* under the title "Sweet Killaloe."

Brian Boru, the eleventh century King of Munster, later to become High King of Ireland, lived in my native town of Killaloe, Co. Clare at Kincora. Brian Boru's fort, on the banks of the River Shannon, is today a tourist attraction. I'm proud to have been born and raised in this historic town. I have fond memories of friends who lived there, including poet Jack Noonan, who penned the following lines in his poem, "Lovely Killaloe":

> Tho' more than tears and lonely years now lie between us two
> I love you still. I always will. My lovely Killaloe.

Father Fielding's Favourite (Jig)

Music collector Captain Francis O'Neill collected this tune from Father Fielding, a flute player who lived in Chicago around the turn of the last century. A version of the tune can be found in O'Neill's *The Dance Music of Ireland: 1001 Gems.*

Master fiddler and virtuoso Seán Maguire, along with pianist Eileen Lane, recorded this jig on a 78-rpm record at the end of the 1950s. Seán Maguire's brilliant fiddle playing influenced many musicians of my generation, not only in Ireland but also in Scotland, Cape Breton and French Canada. Seán still continues to amaze and influence a whole new generation of musicians through recordings, master classes and a busy concert schedule.

Forget Me Not (Reel)

The late Larry Redican, who lived in New York City, was a great fiddle player and composer. Born in Co. Roscommon, Larry grew up in Dublin and moved to Toronto before settling in

New York. He wrote many fine Irish tunes, including this one. I have fond memories of Larry (during one of his visits to Ireland) sitting in my kitchen, playing tune after tune and relating stories to me about the Irish music scene in New York. I had always admired Larry's playing and I was particularly fascinated with his unique bowing. I asked him if he would teach me his style of executing the bow treble. He promised to do so whenever we would next meet. Unfortunately we never did meet again nor did we have an opportunity to work together. Sadly, Larry died suddenly after playing a few tunes at a céilí in Minneola, Long Island, New York.

The Good Woman's Lament for O'Connell (Air)

In 1897 the Dublin Feis Ceóil Association offered a prize for the discovery of previously unpublished Irish melodies. The tunes could be submitted in manuscript form or sung, whistled, or performed on any instrument. The intent of the Feis Ceóil Association was to collect a number of tunes that might otherwise be lost or forgotten. "The Good Woman's Lament for O'Connell" was written down from the playing of John Kenny who, like his wife Brigid, played the fiddle. The tune was published by the Dublin Feis Ceóil Association in 1914 in a collection of eighty-five tunes.

The name Mrs. Brigid Kenny is well known to traditional Irish musicians. Tunes bearing her name are often played in music circles. The legendary fiddler Michael Coleman recorded "Mrs. Kenny's Waltz" and "Mrs. Kenny's Barndance," both tunes attributed to Mrs. Kenny.

The Great Northern Bands (March)

I have known this march for many years, and remember hearing it played by some of the great bands from the north of Ireland on Radio Telefís Éireann's *Céilí House* in the 1960s. I also remember hearing the tune played in céilí band competitions at the All-Ireland fleadhanna cheoil in the '60s and '70s. It had been suggested to me that the tune might be a composition of Brian O'Kane's, a piano accordionist who played with the famous Siamsa Céilí Band. I recently contacted Brian and he assured me that he did not compose the tune. Musicians I have spoken with, including Brian, Joe Burke, flutist Larry Nugent and my brother Michael (a piano player), agree that the tune is most likely associated with the music of céilí bands from the northern counties of Ireland. For lack of a title, we have named the tune "The Great Northern Bands."

The Hare in the Corn (Jig)

For forty years, my good friend Dr. Ciarán MacMathúna presented two programmes of traditional Irish music and song on Irish radio, *Ceolta Tire* on Sunday afternoons and *A Job of Journeywork* on Tuesday evenings. Ciarán traveled the length and breadth of Ireland recording the music and songs of the country people. He then brought these recordings back to the Dublin studios and presented them to the nation. It was on one of Ciarán's programmes that I first heard "The Hare in the Corn."

Ciarán did not have to travel very far to record this lovely tune. It was played for him by a group of Dublin based musicians collectively known as the Castle Céilí Band. This great band had many fine musicians among its ranks, including Seán Keane, Mick O'Connor, Paddy O'Brien (Co. Offaly), John Kelly, Joe Ryan, Bridie Lafferty, John Dwyer, Bernard Carey and Michael Tubridy. My good friend James Keane was the original accordionist with the "Castle," but he was living and performing in New York City when Ciarán recorded this jig.

Hickey's (Reel)

When Ciarán MacMathúna visited North America in the early 1960s to collect music for his radio series, *American Journeywork,* Co. Kerry fiddler Paddy Cronin played this reel for him in Boston. Paddy told Ciarán that he learned this tune from his teacher, Pádraig O'Keeffe, the Sliabh Luachra fiddle master. Paddy also told Ciarán that Pádraig always called the tune "Hickey's Reel."

Humours of Castle Bernard (Hornpipe)

I often heard this hornpipe played on Radio Telefís Éireann in the 1960s. This tune could have been named for either of the two castles in Ireland named for the Bernard family. Castle Bernard in Co. Cork is the old castle of the O'Mahony Clan, and was formerly known as Castle Mahon. The Bernards acquired it in the seventeenth century and eventually renamed it Castle Bernard. Castle Bernard in Co. Offaly (subsequently known as Kinnitty Castle) was the home of the sixth Lord Decies. The castle was sold around 1950 and is now a forestry center. A version of this tune can also be found in O'Neill's *The Dance Music of Ireland: 1001 Gems.*

Jimmy O'Brien's (Jig)

The first two parts of this four-part jig were very popular when I was a "young fella." I heard them played in Newtown, Nenagh, Co. Tipperary, during my visits to the home of Dinny O'Brien, father of legendary accordionist Paddy O'Brien. The O'Brien homestead was affectionately known as "The Bridge," and I often spent my Saturdays there listening to Dinny play the fiddle and tell stories about his son Paddy, who at that time was living in New York City. The jig was a particular favourite of Dinny's but he did not have a name for it.

I later came upon an old 78-rpm recording on the Okeh label (the General Phonograph Corporation of New York) of Sligo fiddle master James Morrison playing these same two parts of the tune. Morrison named the tune "Mist on the Meadow." My long time friend, accordionist Larry Gavin, who lives in Tulla, Co. Clare, told me that the jig was given to Captain O'Neill by a piper who lived in Chicago in the 1870s. It was included in O'Neill's *The Dance Music of Ireland: 1001 Gems* as a three-part tune. Larry told me that a version of the tune also appears as a four-part jig in O'Neill's *Waifs and Strays of Gaelic Melody.*

To add to the confusion about the title and number of parts in this tune, my good friend Mary Lamey recently gave me a new CD recording of her late father's music, *Full Circle*, released by Rounder Records. On it, master Cape Breton fiddler Bill Lamey plays a beautiful three-part version of this jig. Bill's version, named "The Cossy Jig," can be found in Niel Gow's second collection of tunes, published in Scotland in 1788. Whatever its name and whatever its origins, it remains a great tune. Enjoy playing it !!

John Kelly's Concertina Reel (Reel)

This is another tune I first heard on Ciarán MacMathúna's *Ceolta Tíre* and *A Job of Journeywork* programmes. The tune was played by the Castle Céilí Band. The late John Kelly, master fiddler and concertina player, was originally from West Clare, lived in Dublin, and was a member of this great group of Dublin musicians. John also played with Ceoltóirí Laighean, another Dublin ensemble that included his son, master fiddler James Kelly. John Kelly's enormous contribution to the revival of Irish traditional music will forever be remembered. He was a guiding light and an inspiration to many musicians, including Seán Ó Riada. John was an original member of Ó Riada's Ceoltóirí Chualann.

I have one special memory of John Kelly. Both of us were competing in an Oireachtas Céilí Band competition in the Mansion House in Dublin. John was with the Castle Céilí Band and I was playing with the Kilfenora. During the Kilfenora's performance one of my fiddle strings broke and I had to stop playing as the band continued to finish the tune. John was standing at the back of the hall and he saw what happened. Between selections he walked to the stage and handed me his fiddle so that I could continue to play with the band. That's the kind of gentleman John was!! Always encouraging young musicians. Don't ask who won the competition, (*whisper...*) "the Castle."

Kathleen Lawrie's Wedding (Reel)

The home of Dr. and Mrs. Robert Lawrie was, for me and for many of my musical colleagues, the "heart" of traditional Irish music in Birmingham, England. Mrs. Lawrie was a fiddle player from Roscommon who chaired Birmingham's Comhaltas chapter in the 1960s and early 1970s, and who also led the Birmingham Céilí Band during that period. Her daughters Kathleen and Margaret, both excellent musicians, were members of the band, and during our youth we met each other at the fleadhanna and enjoyed many hours playing and discussing music together. Kathleen was a relentless champion in every piano and piano accordion contest she entered. I have fond memories of visits to the Lawrie family home and recall music sessions with Paul Brock, Séamus Shannon, Brendan Mulvihill, Catherine McEvoy and others. The great flute player Josie McDermott from Co. Roscommon was among the frequent musical visitors as well.

When Kathleen married Tommy Boyle of Co. Tyrone (Tommy was the drummer with the Birmingham Céilí Band), Josie composed this reel as a tribute to her. Flute player Marcus Ó Murchú from Belfast has recorded a lovely version of this tune (in a style reminiscent of Josie's playing) on his CD *Ó Bhéal go Béal,* distributed by Cló Iar-Chonnachta.

The last time I saw Josie was in September of 1984 when he was visiting Boston. He performed many of his own compositions during a concert at the Village Coach House in Brookline, Massachusetts. He had named one of the compositions he played that evening "A Trip to Birmingham," and later that night we enjoyed sharing reminiscences of the great musical times we had spent together in Birmingham at the Lawries' home.

Kathleen O'Shea's or *Ben Hill* (Hornpipe)

I have always associated this tune with Kathleen O'Shea-Maguire from London, England, a former World Champion Irish step dancer. I had the honour of playing this hornpipe for Kathleen when she appeared on Radio Telefís Éireann's *Late Late Show* soon after she had won this prestigious dance competition. My good friend, the legendary accordionist Joe Burke, told me that the late and great Ballinakill fiddle player Aggie White discovered the tune but did not have a name for it. On their way to a performance in the 1960s, Joe and Aggie decided to name it "Ben Hill," a name given to an incline on the road close to the home of Aggie and her husband Séamus Ryan. The Reverend Father P.J. Kelly, a renowned musician and composer who hails from Woodford, near Ballinakill, happens to have composed another tune with the same title.

Almost thirty years have passed since I first played this tune for Kathleen O'Shea. Kathleen now can boast that her daughter Ellie Maguire is also a World Champion Irish step dancer. The tradition lives on!! "Ben Hill," "Kathleen O'Shea's," decide for yourself which title you wish to use! Enjoy the tune.

Kiss Me Sweetheart (Single Jig)

I first heard this tune performed by the Dublin based Loch Gamhna Céilí Band in the early 1960s at a fíor-chéilí organized by the Nenagh, Co. Tipperary branch of Conradh na Gaeilge. Whenever I listen to the reel-to-reel recording I made that night in Nenagh, visions of the dancers, elegantly executing "Briseadh na Carraige," "Pléaráca na Banndan," "Cor na Síóg" and "Cadhp an Chúil Áird" to the great music of the Loch Gamhna, again come to life. A special memory of that same night was watching Paddy O'Brien from Newtown play the accordion with the band. Paddy had just returned to live in Ireland after having spent eight years in New York City.

A version of "Kiss Me Sweetheart" also appears in O'Neill's *The Dance Music of Ireland: 1001 Gems.*

Kiss the Bride (Reel)

I heard this reel played many times on Radio Telefís Éireann in the 1960s. The tune is not played very often now. With its inclusion in this tune book, we hope that it will once again become popular.

The Knockawhinna (Jig)

Concertina and piano-accordion player Micheál Ó hEidhin composed this lovely three-part jig during his years as a student at University College Cork. He named the tune in honour of Knockawhinna, near Rockchapel in Co. Cork, an area well known for its traditional Irish music.

Throughout his life Micheál has devoted himself to the promotion and teaching of traditional Irish music. In his efforts to improve the quality of teaching of the music, he created the Comhaltas Ceoltóirí Éireann diploma course in 1980. In his current position as primary/post primary music inspector with the Department of Education, he has collaborated with Comhaltas and the Royal Irish Academy of Music to create a syllabus and structured set of examinations for young traditional Irish musicians.

Micheál's concertina playing may be heard on a recently-released recording, *Cumar*, distributed by Cló Iar-Chonnachta. He also can be heard playing piano accompaniment for me on the 1966 CCE recording *The Rambles of Kitty*, for which he was also the musical director.

Laurel and I are grateful to Micheál for allowing us to publish this great composition.

Lad O'Beirne's (Reel)

A native of Co. Sligo, James "Lad" O'Beirne lived in New York and often played music with the legendary fiddle master Michael Coleman. Lad was the son of Phillip O'Beirne, who gave a youthful Coleman fiddle lessons before Coleman immigrated to America.

Lad O'Beirne was the composer of some lovely tunes, several of which have been recorded for posterity by other musicians. The CD recording *Milestone at the Garden*, issued by Rounder Records in 1996, features a few tracks of Lad's fiddle playing with his friend Louis E. Quinn, a native of Co. Armagh. There are also recordings of Lad's music in private collections, but unfortunately these are not readily available for the general public to hear and admire. This tune, which bears Lad's name, was written out for me by another renowned fiddle player, Paddy Reynolds from Co. Longford. Paddy, who lives on Staten Island, New York, was friendly with Lad and they, too, often played music together.

Marian McCarthy (Set Dance)

This set dance is a composition of the late Con Foley, a fiddle player (originally from Co. Cork) who lived in Limerick. Con dedicated the tune to Marian McCarthy, an outstanding dancer from that famous city. I frequently played for Marian when she danced in competitions in the late 1960s and early 1970s. It was always a pleasure; she was a lovely dancer with a superb sense of rhythm.

Con Foley was very active in the traditional music scene in counties Tipperary, Clare and

Limerick in the 1960s and 70s. He organized a music club in the town of Shannon, and its membership included some of his fellow employees at the airport, including accordion players Larry Gavin and Dennis Doody, and fiddler, flutist and piper Peadar O'Loughlin. Many a good long night of music was heard and played at this club. There were also many great nights of music at Con's home in Limerick. It was at one of these sessions that I met the great pianist Barbara Magone. Barbara and I recorded "Marian McCarthy" on a Green Linnet CD, *Here and There*. Laurel and I wish to thank Con's son Neil, also a fine fiddle player, for allowing us to publish this tune and another of his father's compositions, "Planxty Penny."

Martin Ansboro's (Reel)

Catherine McEvoy, the great flute player now living in Co. Meath, played and recorded this tune for me during the last visit my family and I had to the home of Dr. and Mrs. Lawrie in Birmingham, England. Visiting also at that time was our good friend and legendary musician and composer, the late Josie McDermott. We played a lot of music during that visit and the ever so generous Josie played many old tunes for us from his own locality, the area in and around the Roscommon/Sligo border. He also played for us some of his own wonderful compositions that we captured on tape.

Catherine was a visiting professor at the Boston College Gaelic Roots Summer School in 1999 and she very kindly played "Martin Ansboro's" for me again, bringing back many memories of my visits to the Lawrie home. The tune is named for Martin Ansboro of Bohola, Co. Mayo.

The Meelick Team (Jig D minor)

Fiddler and accordionist Eddie Kelly composed this tune to celebrate Meelick's victory in a Co. Galway hurling championship in the 1960s. According to Joe Burke, another Meelick hurling team represented Galway against Tipperary in the late nineteenth century. Now living in Co. Roscommon, Eddie grew up near Meelick and Eyrecourt in Co. Galway, an area that has produced many fine hurlers, musicians and composers.

The Meelick Team (Jig E minor)

Eddie told me that when he originally wrote "The Meelick Team" it was in the key of D minor. He later transposed the tune to the key of E minor to better suit the instruments in the local band with which he played.

Mick Collins' Reel (Reel)

My good friend Larry (Lar) Gavin learned this tune from Paddy O'Brien (Co. Tipperary). Lar sent it to me on manuscript paper and when I played it, it reminded me that Paddy had many long-forgotten and rare tunes. Paddy told Lar that Mick Collins was a neighbour of his and that he was always "jigging" this tune. Mick didn't have a name for it so Paddy christened it "Mick Collins'."

Minnie Foster's (Hornpipe)

We don't know who Minnie Foster was, but she must have been a great lady to have this lovely tune named for her. I first heard the tune "Minnie Foster's" played in the home of Dave Collins (brother of fiddlers Kathleen Collins and Daniel Collins of Shanachie Record fame) in the Bronx, New York in 1972. On that occasion it was fiddlers Andy McGann and Paddy Reynolds who played it. Paddy and Andy were part of a musical gathering that included Joe Burke, Séamus MacMathúna (music officer of Comhaltas Ceoltóirí Éireann), master fiddle and flute player John-Joe Gardiner (a neighbour of James Morrison before James immigrated to America), Kevin Burke, Paddy Glackin, and my uncle Paddy Connolly (the first person that I ever saw playing a fiddle). A version of the tune can be found in *Ryan's Mammoth Collection*. Uilleann piper and folk singer Patrick Sky wrote the introduction and historical notes for the most recent edition, published by Mel Bay Publications in 1995. The original collection was published in 1883.

Molly on the Shore (Reel)

This fascinating tune is actually a composite of two reels from Cork, and it has attracted the attention of many different musicians through the years. I learned the first three parts included in this book from the playing of the great uilleann piper Leo Rowsome.

The first two parts of Leo's version come from a tune called "Temple Hill," which can be found in George Petrie's book, *The Complete Collection of Irish Music*. Leo's third part is taken from the tune "Molly on the Shore," also published in the Petrie collection.

The great violinist Fritz Kreisler (1875-1962) is known to have performed and recorded a version of "Molly on the Shore." In keeping with the common practice among classical composers of creating orchestral concert music based upon folk melodies, the English composer Percy Grainger (1882-1961) invented a clever arrangement that juxtaposes all five parts of both tunes.

Laurel and I have chosen to continue the tradition of revising the tune, and we have added an alternative third part that plays on phrases from all three parts of Petrie's "Molly on the Shore."

The Morning Mist (Reel)

Joe Burke composed this lovely tune when he was a teenager. His recollection is that the first part of the tune came to him as he was cycling home from half-eleven mass in Loughrea one Sunday morning. Later in the afternoon when he took out the accordion he made up the second part of the tune. "The Morning Mist" has been played and enjoyed by musicians for many years. We are grateful to Joe for providing us with his variations to the tune and for allowing us to publish and print them in this collection.

The Mountain Top (Reel)

This popular reel was recorded by Paddy Cronin in the 1950s for a 78-rpm released on the Boston Copley label. On this recording, Paddy called the tune "Quinn's," preceding it with the "Doon Reel," which we have also included in this book. (See notes on the "Doon Reel.")

Murphy's (Reel)

Our good friend Jack Coen, master flutist, teacher of champions and National Fellowship award winner, wrote down this tune for fiddle player Larry Reynolds, Laurel and me, and sent it to us about six years ago. Jack had picked up the tune while on holidays in Ireland, and he knew that we would enjoy playing it. The reel was commonly known as "Phil Murphy's," and was named for the great Co. Wexford harmonica player.

On the recent Patrick Street CD, *Live from Patrick Street,* the group plays this tune as part of a three-reel set, the "Raheen Medley." The liner notes mention that the tune came from Dennis "The Weaver" Murphy. I contacted the master fiddler in the group, Mr. Kevin Burke, to inquire if he had any other information about this reel. Kevin e-mailed the following information to me, and with his kind permission we now print his story in these notes. (Thanks for all of the help Kevin, you're a "mine" of information!) Here's Kevin's story:

> Here's my tale – I heard Phil Murphy and his two sons, John and Pip, playing a set of three reels, the first one a local Wexford tune called (according to Phil) "The Raheen Reel." The others had no names as far as I knew and I presumed that they were all tunes local to Wexford so I referred to all three as "The Raheen Medley." I played that set for years, sometimes on my own, sometimes with Jackie Daly, sometimes with Patrick Street. One day Jackie told me that as far as he knew the third reel was not from Wexford but was a tune from Dennis "The Weaver" Murphy, the great Kerry fiddler. John Murphy (Phil's son) later told me that Phil used to call it "The Dingle Reel" because he had heard some lads from Dingle, in Kerry, playing it at a fleadh (but John is pretty sure that "The Dingle Reel" isn't the proper name, Phil just called it that for convenience). So now, there's the Kerry connection which would also suggest that it is indeed one of Dennis Murphy's tunes!"

Phil Murphy's harmonica playing may be heard on Kevin's *Up Close* album, released on the Green Linnet label in 1984.

No Surrender (Jig March)

"No Surrender" appears in P.W. Joyce's book, *Ancient Irish Music* in the key of C. According to Joyce, the melody was used as the marching tune at the yearly celebration of the shutting and opening of the Gates of Derry. He believed it to be well known among musicians in some parts of Ulster but scarcely heard in other provinces. The tune also appears in the key of D under the title, "Old Derry March" in the book, *Allan's Irish Fiddler, Containing 120 Reels, Jigs, Hornpipes and Set Dances*. The melody is related to the song, "Beidh Ríl Againn," which I learned in primary school. The song may be found in leaflet 31 of Colm Ó Lochlainn's publication, *An Claisceadal* (duilleachán 31, 1940).

More than thirty years have passed since Seán Óg Ó Tuama wrote down for me on manuscript paper this version of the tune "No Surrender" and his version of "Pigeon on the Gate" (also in this volume). Seán Óg Ó Tuama was born in Cork City into an Irish speaking family. He was involved in the Republican movement from an early age, and was also very active in the Gaelic League movement. He was in prison, serving time for his Republican activities in the Curragh of Kildare, when he was elected president of the Gaelic League for the 1941-1942 (two-year) term.

Seán learned many songs from his mother, and he learned music from Professor Aloys Fleischmann at University College Cork. He taught and led An Claisceadal, a choral group from Cork that broadcast weekly on Raidió Éireann for eleven years. One hundred and twenty of the songs he taught were published in a series of twelve booklets called *An Chóisir Cheoil* (The Musical Party). Seán Óg Ó Tuama was one of the most influential forces in the rising popularity of Gaelic song in the second half of the twentieth century.

The Old Blackbird (Hornpipe)

There are many versions of the tune "The Blackbird." This version, "The Old Blackbird," is distinct from the more commonly heard tune, and I was uncertain of its origin. Because I knew that there were words to the melody I contacted my friend Frank Harte of Dublin, a great singer and authority on old Irish songs. Over the phone, Frank kindly sang to me a song called "The Royal Blackbird," based on the same tune as the "Old Blackbird" hornpipe included in this book. The following is the first verse of the song:

> One fair summer's morning of soft recreation,
> I heard a fair maiden a making great moan.
> With sighing and sobbing and sad lamentation,
> And saying my blackbird most royal has flown.
> My thoughts they deceive me, reflection it grieves me,
> And I am overburdened with sad misery,
> Yet if death it should blind me as true love inclines me,
> My Blackbird I'd seek out wherever he be.

Frank also sent us information about the political and historical significance of the song. Laurel and I are honoured and grateful for Frank's willingness to share his knowledge with us.

According to Frank, it is common in the Irish ballad singing tradition to ascribe the names of animals, particularly birds, to political leaders. In this song, "the blackbird" is an allegorical reference to Bonnie Prince Charlie, and the words of the song lament his defeat and exile in France. The maiden in the story is the personification of Ireland, and it is she who expresses her sorrow that her "royal blackbird" has flown.

The song also appears under the title, "The Blackbird" in P.W. Joyce's published collection, *Old Irish Folk Music and Songs*.

The Old Cross (March)

Céilí dances were very popular in the 1960s. Bands were formed throughout the country to play music for these social gatherings. One such band was the Old Cross Céilí Band from near Dungannon in Co. Tyrone. This band performed a number of times on *Céilí House*, hosted by Seán Ó Murchú. The Old Cross Céilí Band played this march as their signature tune to begin and end their performances. I recall that Pat Hamill (fiddle), Mickey McNally (piano), John Clancy (double bass), and Tom Quinn (accordion and banjo) played with the band on one of these broadcasts. We don't have a name for the tune but we think "The Old Cross" fits it well.

The Old Dudeen (Reel)

Whenever I play or hear the tune "The Old Dudeen" (*Dúidín*), I am reminded of what was for me one of the most exciting and memorable moments of my musical life. My thoughts go back to a concert many years ago when, for my first and only time, I saw and heard the legendary fiddler Paddy Killoran. As part of his performance that evening, Paddy played this reel. In what would today be considered unusual in a concert, he chose to play only reels for his set. I still cherish and treasure the recording I made that evening, over forty years ago, of the master's music.

Today Paddy's 1949 recording of "The Old Dudeen" and "On the Road to Lurgan," two reels he played together that night in West Clare, can be heard on the 1996 Rounder Records CD *Milestone at the Garden,* produced by Dick Spottswood and Philippe Varlet.

Note: A *dúidín* is a short-stemmed clay smoking pipe that was common in Ireland.

Old Ireland a Long Farewell (Air)

This is another tune published by the Dublin Feis Ceóil Association in their 1914 collection. It was submitted to the association for consideration by Mr. James Whiteside. For further information on the association's book, see the notes to "The Good Woman's Lament for O'Connell."

O'Reilly's Greyhound (Reel)

My brother, accordionist Martin Connolly, gave me the name for this tune. A version of it appears in O'Neill's *The Dance Music of Ireland: 1001 Gems.*

Fiddle player and guitarist Randal Bays performed a version of this tune for us when he visited Boston College recently. He learned his version of the tune from the legendary East Clare fiddle player P.J. Hayes, who called it "Murphy's Greyhound."

Paddy Fahey's (Reel)

One of the most prolific composers of our time is fiddler Paddy Fahey from Co. Galway. He has composed almost seventy tunes, and his compositions have been in circulation for years although some, too, have been forgotten. Down through the years musicians have been playing and recording Paddy's tunes, sometimes without even knowing they were his compositions. Paddy never did name his tunes, so musicians just called them "Paddy Fahey's." In 1966 I had the honour of recording two of Paddy's reels for Comhaltas Ceóltoirí Éireann's (CCE) first long-playing record, *The Rambles of Kitty.* There are plans underway to re-issue this historic recording as a CD to commemorate the golden anniversary of the organization. Laurel and I are indebted to Mr. Fahey for allowing us to publish this lovely reel, which I first heard played by accordion master John Bowe from Birr, Co. Offaly.

Paddy Kelly's (Reel)

"The Aughrim Slopes," as they were affectionately known, was one of the finest céilí bands of its day. Their unmistakable "solid-as-a-rock" sound can be heard on recordings made in the 1940s. The passion and love that these musicians had for their music, their rhythm and phrasing and "feel for the tunes," are all woven together on these wonderful and rare 78-rpm records. One can also hear the beautiful free-flowing style of the fiddles, played by Jack Mulcaire, Paddy Fahey and Paddy Kelly. Mr. Kelly is remembered as a wonderful tunesmith and his compositions, like those of Paddy Fahey, have been recorded by many musicians, including yours truly. In 1993, when Jack Coen, Martin Mulhaire, Felix Dolan and I recorded our CD *Warming Up* for Green Linnet Records, we included this lovely Paddy Kelly composition on the recording.

Pigeon on the Gate (Single Jig)

This tune was given to me by the late Seán Óg Ó Tuama (see notes for "No Surrender"). There are a number of versions of the tune "Pigeon on the Gate," and it is most commonly played as a reel. The melody in this publication appears as a single jig, but one can hear the musical threads of the reel running through it.

Planxty Penny (Set Dance)

This set dance is a composition of the great Limerick fiddle player Con Foley (see notes for

"Marian McCarthy"). Con named this tune in honour of Celine Penny, who directed a dancing school in Limerick City during the time I lived there in the 1960s and 1970s.

The Second Wedding (Reel)

When Paddy O'Brien and I met in 1974 to choose the tunes for the Comhaltas Ceoltóirí Éireann recording *The Banks of the Shannon* (an extended-playing record with six tracks), "The Second Wedding" was one of the tunes we considered including. I still enjoy listening to a cassette tape I made of Paddy playing this tune as he read it from O'Neill's *The Dance Music of Ireland: 1001 Gems*. The tape also includes a version he learned from his father, Dinny. It is Dinny O'Brien's version we include in this book.

Green Linnet Records re-issued *The Banks of the Shannon* in 1993 as a CD, with four additional tracks recorded by Dr. Charlie Lennon and myself. The CD also includes some earlier recordings made by Paddy in 1954 for the Columbia Graphophone Company Limited. These recordings were made at his home in Newtown, Nenagh on the night before his departure for New York, where he lived for the next eight years.

Sixmilebridge (Reel)

I first heard this tune played by the Castle Céilí Band on one of Ciarán MacMathúna's radio broadcasts. It was the same programme on which they played "The Hare in the Corn" (see notes for "The Hare in the Corn"). A hornpipe version of this tune can be found in O'Neill's *The Dance Music of Ireland: 1001 Gems* under the title "The Banks of the Ilen."

The Spindle Shanks (Reel)

Accordionist and composer Paddy O'Brien of Co. Offaly (and currently of Minneapolis) identifies the Sligo whistle player James McGettrick as the source of this tune. It was Anne Sheehy-McAuliffe who gave us the tune's title, "The Spindle Shanks." The tune was recorded under that name by Dr. Charlie Lennon on fiddle and Mick O'Connor on flute for the 1981 Comhaltas Ceoltóirí Éireann LP *Lucky in Love*.

The Tempest (Reel)

Like most musicians living in Ireland in the 1960s, I eagerly awaited Ciarán MacMathúna's weekly radio programmes. With reel-to-reel tape recorders, we re-recorded from these broadcasts many lovely tunes and songs that Ciarán had personally collected from musicians and singers around the country. It was on one of these programmes that I first heard this tune played by fiddle masters Joe Ryan and the late John Kelly. Unfortunately, I am not familiar with the tune's history nor do I know the name of its composer. However, from listening to John and Joe's haunting and lonesome rendition, one could easily surmise that the tune originated in West Clare.

The Thrush in the Bush (Jig)

I have always associated this tune with fiddler, pianist and composer, Josephine Keegan from Co. Armagh. Josephine performed it on fiddle years ago on a Raidió Éireann Irish music programme. She also played it on one of her albums, distributed by the Outlet Recording Company of Belfast. The LP sleeve notes did not identify the composer, but my intuition told me that it was Josephine's composition. I contacted Josephine by phone to inquire if this was the case. She shyly admitted that indeed it was her tune and she also told me she was delighted that we would consider including it in our book. Laurel and I are honoured to have this tune in the book and are grateful to Josephine for her kind permission to publish it.

Aside from the solo fiddle albums that Josephine recorded (to her own piano accompaniment) she can also be heard on recordings made with other masters such as Seán Maguire, Séamus Tansey, Roger Sherlock and Joe Burke.

Tommy Mulhaire's (Jig)

The late Tommy Mulhaire, music teacher and composer, put this lovely jig in circulation around 1958. He composed the tune during the time he lived near Eyrecourt in Co. Galway, just before he settled in Galway City. Tommy was father to Martin and Brendan Mulhaire, who (as previously mentioned) have distinguished themselves as exceptional composers. The great Mulhaire tradition of composing music extended not only to Tommy's sons, but also to his nephew, Johnny McEvoy. An internationally known balladeer, Johnny has penned many fine songs that are part of the standard repertory wherever a good Irish ballad is sung.

I have had the pleasure of knowing Tommy Mulhaire since the late 1950s. I have also had the honour of playing music with him at the famous all-star concerts that Jerry Keane organized in Lixnaw, Co. Kerry. Tommy was a gentleman who never failed to encourage young musicians. He was a great teacher of the fiddle, accordion, and other instruments, and he taught Irish music to hundreds of children throughout the west of Ireland.

The last time I saw Tommy we had both changed considerably in the thirty years since we had last met. I said hello and asked if he knew who I was. "You're a Connolly," he said, "...if you're not Martin, you're Séamus."

Biographical Notes:

SÉAMUS CONNOLLY AND LAUREL MARTIN

SÉAMUS CONNOLLY, a native of Killaloe, Co. Clare, Ireland, is one of the world's most respected Irish fiddle players. Born in 1944, Séamus grew up in a home filled with music. Both his parents and his two brothers played traditional music, and Séamus began playing the fiddle at the age of 12. His father encouraged him to listen to the recordings of the famed Co. Sligo fiddler Michael Coleman, later to become one of Séamus' musical heroes.

Séamus' musical upbringing and dedication won him the Irish National Fiddle Championship ten times, along with the coveted Fiddler of Dooney competition. As a member of the Kilfenora Céilí Band, he traveled throughout Ireland and Britain to play for dances, concerts, radio and television. Séamus' first trip to the United States was in 1972, as part of the first Comhaltas Ceoltóirí Éireann (CCE) tour.

In 1976, Séamus immigrated to the United States and settled in the Boston area. In 1977, at the invitation of Larry Reynolds, president of the Boston (Hanafin-Cooley) branch of CCE, Séamus began teaching fiddle to American students, sharing with them the various regional styles of Irish fiddling.

Séamus has had the honour of representing Ireland on three "Masters of the Folk Violin" tours organized by the National Council for the Traditional Arts. He has performed at most major festivals in the United States, and on the *"Folk Masters"* radio series of National Public Radio. As a performer, teacher and lecturer, he has traveled to Australia, Spain, France, England, Canada, Alaska and Ireland. In 1990, Séamus received a Massachusetts Cultural Council Fellowship Award, and from 1990 to 1992, the National Endowment for the Arts awarded him three consecutive grants for the purpose of establishing a formal master/apprentice relationship with fiddle player Laurel Martin.

Released on Green Linnet Records are his two solo CDs, *Notes from my Mind* and *Here and There*. Also available on Green Linnet Records are *Banks of the Shannon* (with accordionist Paddy O'Brien and pianist/composer Charlie Lennon), and *Warming Up* (with accordionist Martin Mulhaire, flutist Jack Coen and pianist Felix Dolan).

Séamus is now director of the Boston College Irish Studies Music, Song and Dance Program. He is also director of the Gaelic Roots Summer School and Festival at Boston College.

For further information about Séamus' recordings or about the Gaelic Roots Summer School, consult the Gaelic Roots website (http://www.bc.edu/gaelicroots).

LAUREL MARTIN, a native of Massachusetts, is one of the new generation of traditional Irish musicians in America who has been inspired by Séamus' music and teaching. She has been playing traditional Irish music since 1980, and from 1990 to 1992 she pursued a formal apprenticeship with Séamus under a grant from the National Endowment for the Arts. She is now sought after as a teacher of Irish fiddle music, and is highly respected for her knowledge and commitment to perpetuating the musical styles of the old masters. Laurel is adjunct professor of Irish Music for the Boston College Irish Studies Program, serves on the Music Department faculty at Phillips Academy in Andover, Massachusetts, and also teaches privately. In January 2002, her accomplishments as a musician and teacher were acknowledged as she was once again awarded a Master Apprentice grant from the Massachusetts Cultural Council, this time as a master teacher for the purpose of instructing her young fiddle student Betsy Sullivan in the old traditional styles.

Séamus and Laurel's master/apprentice relationship has evolved over the years to a partnership, and they continue to play, teach and perform together at concerts, workshops and festivals all over the United States. The joy they share in playing and passing on their music finds its creative expression in this, their first publication, the traditional yet innovative *Forget Me Not: Fifty Memorable Traditional Irish Tunes.*

Photo: Jim Higgins